The Wisdom of
the Midwest

The Wisdom of
the Midwest

Common Sense and Uncommon Genius
From 101 Great Midwesterners

Compiled and Edited by Criswell Freeman

WALNUT GROVE PRESS
(615) 256-8584

ISBN 1-887655-17-4

The ideas expressed in this book are not, in all cases, exact quotations, as some have been edited for clarity and brevity. In all cases, the author has attempted to maintain the speaker's original intent. In some cases, material for this book was obtained from secondary sources, primarily print media. While every effort was made to ensure the accuracy of these sources, the accuracy cannot be guaranteed. For additions, deletions, corrections or clarifications in future editions of this text, please write WALNUT GROVE PRESS.

Printed in the United States of America
Cover Design by Bart Dawson
Typesetting & Page Layout by Sue Gerdes
Edited by Alan Ross and Angela Beasley
2 3 4 5 6 7 8 9 10 • 01 02 03 04

ACKNOWLEDGMENTS
The author gratefully acknowledges the helpful support of Angela Beasley, Dick and Mary Freeman, and Mary Susan Freeman.

For Mark Stone

Teacher, Mentor, Friend

Table of Contents

Introduction

The Midwest is more than America's heartland. It's also our pantry and our workshop. It's where food is grown and machines are made by practical, God-fearing, hard-working people. Chicago, the unofficial capital of the Midwest, is "The City That Works." The same could be said for America's heartland; it works.

The wisdom of the Midwest is, in truth, America's wisdom. It comes from the center, from the heart of our nation. This book features inspiring words of 101 great Midwesterners. From Lincoln and Lindbergh to Truman and Twain, the men and women on these pages have much to share. In solid Midwestern fashion, they praise the dignity of work, the necessity of hope, and the value of a good laugh.

In this book, you will enjoy the humor, inspiration and wisdom of America's heartland. You'll find page after page of common-sense advice. Follow it. Because good Midwestern advice is like the city of Chicago: It works.

1

All-Purpose Advice

Gerald Ford observed, "It's the ordinary people, the straight, the square who account for the great stability and success of our nation." He could have been describing the greatness of the Midwest.

Midwesterners, ever the straight-shooters, will gladly exchange a fair day's work for a fair day's pay. They're not afraid to say "Hello," even if you're new in town. In *Travels with Charley*, John Steinbeck wrote, "Almost on crossing the Ohio line it seemed to me that people were more open and outgoing."

Here, notable Midwesterners share a little neighborly wisdom. This sound advice may seem ordinary, straight, even "square," but that's okay. In America's heartland, "tried and true" always beats "trendy and new."

The past is history. Make the present good, and the past will take care of itself.

Knute Rockne

The greatest mistake you can make in life
is to be continually fearing
you will make one.

Elbert Hubbard

Learn by doing.

John Dewey

Learn to fail intelligently.

Charles F. Kettering

When you blunder,
blunder forward.

Thomas Edison

Discourage litigation.

Abraham Lincoln

Watch for opportunities to let the world
know where you stand.

D. L. Moody

Lose with dignity and win with aplomb.

Dave Winfield

Be like the elephant in a circus parade:
Have thick skin and proceed carefully
on the heels of you predecessor.

Adlai Stevenson

Never go to a doctor whose office plants
have died.

Erma Bombeck

If you want to get rid of somebody,
just tell him something for his own good.

Kin Hubbard

If you wisely invest in beauty,
it will be with you all the days of your life.

Frank Lloyd Wright

Don't be content with your discontent.

Les Brown

It goes without saying that you should never
have more children than you have
car windows.

Erma Bombeck

If you have nothing to say, say nothing.

Mark Twain

Never neglect the opportunity
of keeping your mouth shut.

The Missouri Pharmacist

Stick to what you know.

Warren Buffett

Don't be too proud to take lessons.
I'm not.

Jack Nicklaus

It is easier to stay out
than to get out.

Mark Twain

Never run out of goals.

Earl Nightingale

2

Life

After graduating from the University of Illinois, George Halas briefly played baseball with the New York Yankees. In 1920, young George moved back to his home state and organized a football team for the Staley Starch Company of Decatur. Within a few years, Halas embarked upon a new venture: the Chicago Bears. Along the way, he helped found the National Football League. Halas once observed, "If you live long enough, lots of nice things happen."

In this chapter, great Midwesterners reflect on the elements of a good life. If you take this advice to heart, nice things will happen. Lots of nice things.

Life hurries past,
too strong to stop,
too sweet to lose.

Willa Cather

Time is a circus always packing up
and moving away.

Ben Hecht

Life is like an onion.
You peel it off one layer at a time,
and sometimes you weep.

Carl Sandburg

It's a wonderful world. But you've got to work,
you've got to think, you've got to study.
If you do all these things, it's a pleasure.

Harold Washington

The longer I live, the more beautiful
life becomes.

Frank Lloyd Wright

Time is really the only capital that
    any human being has and the only thing
        he can't afford to lose.

Thomas Edison

Time is the coin of your life.
It is the only coin you have, and only you can
determine how it will be spent. Be careful lest
    you let other people spend it for you.

Carl Sandburg

Time is the least thing we have.

Ernest Hemingway

The best thing about the future is
    that it comes only one day at a time.

Abraham Lincoln

Life is a series of relapses and recoveries.

George Ade

For the cloth of life is woven, you know,
to a pattern hidden under the loom —
a pattern you never see.

Edgar Lee Masters

Change the fabric of your own soul
and your own visions, and you change all.

Vachel Lindsay

Life is like a landscape.
You live in the midst of it, but can describe it
only from the vantage point of distance.

Charles Lindbergh

Life takes on meaning when you become
motivated. Set goals and charge after them
in an unstoppable manner.

Les Brown

The world hates change;
yet, it is the only thing that brings progress.

Charles F. Kettering

Man has always been an explorer.
There's a fascination in thrusting out and
going to new places.

Neil Armstrong

When you're green you're growing;
when you're ripe you rot.

Ray Kroc

Life is like a ten-speed bike. Most of us have
gears we never use.

Charles Schulz

Always be in a state of becoming.

Walt Disney

God is busy with all of us.

Ben Hecht

A baby is God's opinion that
the world should go on.

Carl Sandburg

It takes life to love life.

Edgar Lee Masters

The game is meant to be fun.

Jack Nicklaus

There's nothing funnier than
the human animal.

Walt Disney

Adventure is worthwhile in itself.

Amelia Earhart

The world is wide, and I will not waste
my life in friction when it could be turned
into momentum.

Frances Willard

Life is not meant to be endured,
but enjoyed.

Hubert H. Humphrey

All I can say about life is: Enjoy it.

Bob Newhart

Do not take life too seriously.
You will never get out of it alive.

Elbert Hubbard

Endeavor to live so
that when you die,
even the undertaker
will be sorry.

Mark Twain

Living successfully is a matter
of forming the right habits.

Earl Nightingale

Destiny is not a matter of chance,
it is a matter of choice.

William Jennings Bryan

The future: that period of time in which
our affairs prosper, our friends are true,
and our happiness is assured.

Ambrose Bierce

The past is a bucket of ashes, so live not
in your yesterdays, not just for tomorrow,
but in the here and now.

Carl Sandburg

Age is a case of mind over matter.
    If you don't mind, it doesn't matter.

Jack Benny

If life were fair Elvis would be alive
    and all the impersonators would be dead.

Johnny Carson

We're all cremated equal.

Jane Ace

3

Attitude

Harry Truman grew up on a farm in Independence, Missouri. As a hard-working farm boy, young Truman acquired a healthy dose of Midwestern common sense. Lessons learned in boyhood prepared Harry for the difficult decisions that lay ahead.

Truman was once asked to give his opinion about positive and negative attitudes. He responded, "A pessimist is one who makes difficulties out of his opportunities. An optimist is one who makes opportunities out of his difficulties."

If you're in need of an attitude adjustment, read on. You'll discover a truth that Harry Truman learned many years ago: When it comes to turning difficulties into opportunities, the buck stops here.

I've never seen a monument erected
to a pessimist.

Paul Harvey

Think of what you can do with what there is.

Ernest Hemingway

You can't have a better tomorrow
if you are always thinking about yesterday.

Charles F. Kettering

If you think small, you'll stay small.

Ray Kroc

Cultivate cheerfulness.

Knute Rockne

The things that empower you —
the possibilities — come from within.

Les Brown

Character is the result of two things —
mental attitude and
the way we spend our time.

Elbert Hubbard

Attitude is not just the way you think —
it's the way you live.

Fielding Yost

Self-inspiration is the most important
ingredient for success.

W. Clement Stone

Treat pain and rage as visitors.

Ben Hecht

Focus on remedies, not faults.

Jack Nicklaus

Always have a next great goal.

Alan Kulwicki

To be energetic, act energetic.

W. Clement Stone

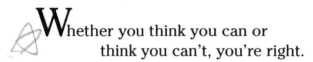Whether you think you can or
think you can't, you're right.

Henry Ford

Perfection is impossible. But striving for it
is what counts.

Dan Gable

He started to sing as he tackled the thing
that couldn't be done,
and he did it.

Edgar A. Guest

Confidence is contagious.
So is the lack of confidence.

Vince Lombardi

Concentration is a fine antidote to anxiety.

Jack Nicklaus

God gave man the ability to forget,
which is one of the greatest attributes.
People who go around "keeping score"
are miserable people.

Hubert H. Humphrey

My interest is in the future, because
I am going to spend the rest of my life there.

Charles F. Kettering

4

Happiness

During his tenure at the University of Chicago, Mortimer Adler helped design the *Great Books*, an encyclopedic compendium of Western thought. Adler, himself a noted philosopher, observed, "The modern understanding of happiness is too often confused with pleasure, satisfaction, or having a good time." Adler's advice was straightforward: "Have a moral aim of leading a whole good life — by building it the way one builds the parts of a play."

Another noted Midwestern thinker, poet Mark Van Doren, seemed to add a footnote to Adler's words when he advised, "It takes courage to be happy."

If you're honestly seeking "a whole good life," consider the sensible advice that follows. And remember that with courage and insight, it's never too late for a happy ending.

Happiness is a matter of your own doing.
You can be happy or you can be unhappy.
It's just according to the way
you look at things.

Walt Disney

Generate happiness within yourself.

Ernie Banks

A man cannot be comfortable
without his own approval.

Mark Twain

The curious paradox is that when I accept
myself just as I am, then I change.

Carl Rogers

Most folks are about
as happy as they make
up their minds to be.

Abraham Lincoln

Guilt: the gift that keeps on giving.

Erma Bombeck

If you aren't happy in one place, chances are
you won't be happy in another place.

Ernie Banks

A new town was only the same town
in a different place.

Susan Glaspell

The disease we all have and fight against
all our lives is, of course, the disease of self.
Let any man look too much upon his own life,
and everything becomes a mess.

Sherwood Anderson

The best way to cheer yourself up
is to cheer up somebody else.

Mark Twain

Kids should have enough money to be able
to do what they want, to learn what they
want, but not enough money to do nothing.

Warren Buffett

It's pretty hard to tell what
does bring happiness. Poverty and wealth
have both failed.

Kin Hubbard

I have discovered the secret formula
for a carefree old age: ICR = FI.
If you can't recall it, forget it.

Goodman Ace

It takes a heap o' lovin' in a house
to make it a home.

Edgar A. Guest

Happiness is accomplishing something
you didn't think you could do.

Ring Lardner

Don't go out looking for happiness.
Happiness is a by-product.

Johnny Carson

Happiness is not a tangible thing,
it's a by-product — a by-product
of achievement.

Ray Kroc

To achieve happiness, we should make
certain we are never without
an important goal.

Earl Nightingale

To find what one is fitted to do and
to secure an opportunity to do it
is the key to happiness.

John Dewey

This is happiness: to be dissolved
into something complete and great.

Willa Cather

Happiness is contagious.

Hubert H. Humphrey

5

Midwestern Wisdom

Edgar Watson Howe founded *The Daily Globe* in Atchison, Kansas. In the closing years of the 19th century, Howe's editorials were widely reprinted in American newspapers, thus spreading the gospel of Midwestern horse-sense to millions of readers.

The best Midwestern wisdom is build on the firm foundation of common sense. As Howe once noted, "A philosophy requiring a large volume is too much; a hundred pages is enough."

You won't need a translator to understand the quotations on the following pages, and that's good. Sometimes, our most important lessons are the simple ones. But simple lessons can be difficult to apply since "the good life" is easier to articulate than to fabricate. Turn the page for some life-changing ideas: applications gladly accepted.

There is the silence of age, too full
    of wisdom for the tongue to utter it.
Edgar Lee Masters

Education is not preparation for life.
    Education is life itself.
John Dewey

The purpose of learning is growth, and
our minds, unlike our bodies, can continue
    growing as long as we live.
Mortimer Adler

Never stop the educational process.
Alan Kulwicki

Absorb ideas from every source.
Thomas Edison

Knowledge is not power.
It is potential power. What's needed is
the ability to motivate yourself to do
what you *know* needs doing.

W. Clement Stone

Study men, not historians.

Harry S. Truman

The art of teaching is the art
of assisting discovery.

Mark Van Doren

Man has much to learn from nature.

Walt Disney

Time is a great teacher.

Carl Sandburg

Tomorrow comes to us at midnight
        very clean. It's perfect when it arrives,
        and it puts itself in our hands and hopes
        we've learnt something from yesterday.

John Wayne

The only people who don't change their minds
        are incompetent or dead.

Everett Dirksen

To get anywhere, a man must have
        a certain amount of intelligent ignorance.

Charles F. Kettering

The only things worth learning are
        the things you know after you learn it all.

Harry S. Truman

The trouble with the world is not that
        people know so little, but that they know
        so many things that ain't so.

Mark Twain

A closed mind is a dying man.

Edna Ferber

Not to engage in the pursuit of ideas is
to live like ants instead of like men.

Mortimer Adler

There is no force so powerful as an idea
whose time has come.

Everett Dirksen

The fear of ideas makes us impotent
and ineffective.

William O. Douglas

The best thinking has been done in solitude.
The worst has been done in turmoil.

Thomas Edison

A good scare is worth more
than good advice.

Edgar Watson Howe

The man who does not read good books
has no advantage over the man
who can't read them.

Mark Twain

The only thing new in this world
is the history you don't know.

Harry S. Truman

Thinking is one thing they've never been
able to tax.

Charles F. Kettering

I have learned a great deal from listening carefully. Most people never listen.

Ernest Hemingway

Towering genius disdains a beaten path.

Abraham Lincoln

Genius must ever walk alone.

George Ade

The problem when solved will be simple.

Sign In General Motors Research Laboratory

Anyone who stops learning is old,
whether at twenty or eighty. Anyone who
keeps learning stays young. The greatest
thing in life is to keep your mind young.

Henry Ford

Technology does not improve the quality
of life; it improves the quality of things.
Improving the quality of life requires
the application of wisdom.

Neil Armstrong

Lord, deliver me from the man who never
makes a mistake, and also from the man
who makes the same mistake twice.

William Mayo

Excesses ultimately, inevitably,
are their own undoing.

Paul Harvey

The truth is more important than the facts.

Frank Lloyd Wright

What I learned growing up is
that we have power over words,
not the other way around.

Tim Allen

Thoughts are acrobats, agile and
quite often untrustworthy.

Bess Streeter Aldrich

You can tell the size of a man by the size
of the thing it takes to make him mad.

Adlai Stevenson

Egotism is the anesthetic that lulls
the pain of stupidity.

Frank Leahy

Your head never begins to swell until
your mind stops growing.

Alan Kulwicki

Never let schooling interfere
with education.

Mark Twain

I think that I think; therefore, I think
that I am.

Ambrose Bierce

Always keep an
open mind and a
compassionate heart.

Phil Jackson

6

Courage

Atchison, Kansas, the home of Edgar Watson Howe, was also the birthplace of Amelia Earhart. In 1932, Earhart became the first woman aviator to make a solo crossing of the Atlantic. After her flight, Amelia warned, "Courage is the price life extracts for peace."

On the pages that follow, the benefits of bravery are discussed by noteworthy Midwesterners. Like Earhart, these men and women have learned that cowardice extracts a terrible price, but courage is its own reward.

Everything is possible to him who dares.

Albert Goodwill Spalding

Live fearlessly.

Oprah Winfrey

A man's doubts and fears
are his worst enemies.

William Wrigley, Jr.

Fear is an illusion.

Michael Jordan

Courage is being scared to death and saddling up anyway.

John Wayne

To sin by silence when they should protest
makes cowards out of men.

Abraham Lincoln

I refuse to worry about more than one thing
at a time.

Ray Kroc

I have a new philosophy. I'm only going
to dread one day at a time.

Charlie Brown

Cartoon Character by Charles Schulz

There can be no courage
unless you're scared.

Eddie Rickenbacker

Courage is grace under pressure.

Ernest Hemingway

Courage is resistance to fear,
  mastery of fear — not absence of fear.

Mark Twain

As a cure for worry,
      work is better than whiskey.

Thomas Edison

It's better to be a lion for a day
      than a sheep all your life.

Sister Elizabeth Kenny

The first and great commandment is: Don't let them scare you.

Elmer Davis

7

Hope

The Midwest boasts more than its fair share of farmers, industrialists, inventors and dreamers. What do these widely disparate groups have in common? They all depend mightily on the power of hope.

In *The Count of Monte Cristo*, Alexandre Dumas wrote, "All human wisdom is summed up in two words — wait and hope." Dumas, of course, was a French novelist and playwright, unfamiliar with America's heartland. He probably never plowed a field or shucked an ear of corn. But, with an attitude like that, Alexandre Dumas would have made a darn good farmer.

Act as though it were impossible to fail.

Dorthea Brande

The future is not ominous, but a promise.
It surrounds the present like a halo.

John Dewey

Never let hope elude you.
That's life's biggest fumble.

Bob Zuppke

To me, faith is not worrying.

John Dewey

Belief in a thing makes it happen.

Frank Lloyd Wright

Horatio Alger still lives
and the American dream is still good.

Paul Harvey

There comes a time
when you have to drop your burdens
to fight for your dreams.

Les Brown

Don't put a ceiling on your dreams.

Dave Winfield

Nothing happens unless it is first a dream.

Carl Sandburg

All our dreams can come true — if we have the courage to pursue them.

Walt Disney

<u>8</u>

Action

From time to time, a towering figure springs from America's heartland and dramatically changes the way the world behaves. Abraham Lincoln relieved America of the burden of slavery. The Wright Brothers taught us to fly. And Henry Ford transformed transportation.

Chicago-born Walt Disney revolutionized the light-hearted world of cartoons and, along the way, changed the way the world takes vacations. First, in 1928, Disney introduced us to a cheerful creation named Mickey Mouse. Then, in 1937, he produced the first full-length cartoon feature film: *Snow White and the Seven Dwarfs*. Finally, in 1955, with his success already assured, Disney took another gamble by opening the first modern-day theme park: Disneyland.

Walt said, "If you can dream it, you can do it." The following quotations suggest various methods by which we may translate our dreams into reality.

Today is when everything that's going
to happen from now on begins.

Harvey Firestone, Jr.

Never mistake motion for action.

Ernest Hemingway

Action is the sole medium of expression
for ethics.

Jane Addams

You can achieve only that which you will do.

George Halas

When you know what you ought to do,
but you don't feel like doing it, do it *now*.

W. Clement Stone

Most people spend more time and energy going around problems than trying to solve them.

Henry Ford

Ask yourself, "Where will I be 10 years from now if I keep doing what I am doing?"

W. Clement Stone

You'll never stub your toe while you're
standing still. The faster you go, the more
chance there is of stubbing your toe but the
more chance you have of getting somewhere.

Charles F. Kettering

And of all glad words of prose and rhyme,
the gladdest are, "Act while
there yet is time."

Franklin Pierce Adams

My message to you is this:
Be courageous. Have faith. Go forward!

Thomas Edison

I walk slowly, but I never walk backwards.

Abraham Lincoln

Sometimes you have to ride the fence
   awhile until you find where the gates are.
Eva Bowring

Carry the battle to them.
      Don't let them bring it to you.
Harry S. Truman

Things may come to those who wait,
   but only the things left by those who hustle.
Abraham Lincoln

People are always neglecting something
         they can do by trying to do
         something they can't.
Edgar Watson Howe

Thinking without constructive action
becomes a disease. Idleness warps the mind.
Henry Ford

Make sure you don't die waiting
    for prosperity to come.

Lee Iacocca

To escape criticism — do nothing,
    say nothing, be nothing.

Elbert Hubbard

Don't be afraid to fail.
    Be afraid not to try.

Michael Jordan

You can't steal second if you don't take
    your foot off first.

Mike Todd

You can't build a reputation
    on what you're going to do.

Henry Ford

The most important history is the history we make today.

Henry Ford

9

Success

Automotive pioneer Charles Kettering once observed, "The Wright Brothers flew through the smoke screen of impossibility." For Kettering, himself a great innovator, "impossible" was a four-letter word.

Another Midwesterner who flew through the smoke screen of impossibility was an Ohioan named Neil Armstrong. After taking his first step on the lunar surface, Armstrong spoke for all of us on earth when he announced, "That's one small step for a man, one giant leap for mankind."

When we summon the courage to exchange small steps for giant leaps, success becomes our traveling companion. In this chapter, notable Midwesterners encourage us to shoot for the moon.

To succeed, one must be creative
and persistent.

John H. Johnson

More men fail through lack of purpose
than lack of talent.

Billy Sunday

Goal-setting is a continuous process.
As you reach one goal, you set the next.

Dave Winfield

The price of success is dedication, hard work
and an unremitting devotion to the things
you want to see happen.

Frank Lloyd Wright

Your own resolution to succeed
is more important than any other thing.

Abraham Lincoln

Opportunity knocks once at every man's door and then keeps on knocking.

George Ade

If money is your hope for security
in this world, you will not have it.
The only real security is a reserve
of knowledge, experience and ability.

Henry Ford

Success is not the result of making money.
Making money is the result of success.

Earl Nightingale

People who make their object to get as much
as possible are always clutching emptiness.

Rudolf Dreikurs

Success has nothing to do with what
you gain in life or accomplish for yourself.
It's what you do for others.

Danny Thomas

We trust that God is on our side. It is more
important that we are on God's side.

Abraham Lincoln

Did you ever have a goal and still not know
where you were going? I knew I wasn't going
to stay where I was, but I wasn't sure
where I was going.

Joe Louis

Success is the progressive realization
of a worthy goal.

Earl Nightingale

Virtually nothing comes out right
the first time. Failures, repeated failures, are
the guideposts on the road to achievement.

Charles F. Kettering

If I take care of my character,
my reputation will take care of itself.

D. L. Moody

You can't escape the responsibility
of tomorrow by evading it today.

Abraham Lincoln

Get a good idea and stay with it. Dog it,
and work at it until it's done, and done right.

Walt Disney

Racing is like life.
If you get up one more time than you fall,
you'll make it through.

Alan Kulwicki

Our greatest weakness lies in giving up.
The most certain way to succeed is to
always try just one more time.

Thomas Edison

Nobody who ever gave his best regretted it.

George Halas

I failed my way to success.

Thomas Edison

Before everything else, getting ready
   is the secret of success.

Henry Ford

First, master the fundamentals.

Larry Bird

The ability to concentrate and use time well
   is everything.

Lee Iacocca

Give me a man who says this one thing I do,
   and not these fifty things I dabble in.

D. L. Moody

I can't imagine a person becoming
a success who doesn't give this game of life
   everything he's got.

Walter Cronkite

Success

It's not how good you are that's important.
It's how good you can be.

Kevin McHale

The will to succeed is important,
but what's even more important
is the will to prepare.

Bobby Knight

Inches make a champion, and the champion
makes his own luck.

Red Blaik

Winning isn't everything,
but wanting to win is.

Vince Lombardi

I don't think winning means anything
in particular. It's the satisfaction you get
from knowing you did your best.

Bonnie Blair

The excellent becomes the permanent.

Jane Addams

Every great achievement is the story
of a flaming heart.

Harry S. Truman

Work for quality, not quantity
or quick money.

Walt Disney

Coming together is a beginning.
Keeping together is progress.
Working together is success.

Henry Ford

Success: the one unpardonable sin
against one's fellows.

Ambrose Bierce

Winners never remember
and losers never forget.

Everett Dirksen

A winner never quits
and a quitter never wins.

Knute Rockne

Show me a thoroughly satisfied man —
and I will show you a failure.

Thomas Edison

You're never a loser until you quit trying.

Mike Ditka

The best place to succeed is where you are
with what you've got.

Charles M. Schwab

To be good at anything,
you must be a nonconformist.

Earl Nightingale

There are people who want to be
everywhere at once and they get nowhere.

Carl Sandburg

The secret to my success?
I get up earlier than most.

Paul Harvey

To be "normal" seems shockingly repellent
to me. I see neither hope nor comfort
in sinking to that level.

Karl Menninger

It's difficult to excel at something
you don't truly enjoy.

Jack Nicklaus

Every man is the architect
of his own fortunes, but the neighbors
superintend the construction.

George Ade

There are no shortcuts
in life — only those
we imagine.

Frank Leahy

10

Others

One of the greatest gifts we can share is the gift of laughter. John William Carson did exactly that. Born in Corning, Iowa, Johnny Carson studied journalism at Nebraska before embarking upon a career in entertainment. In 1962, he began a thirty-year run as host of *The Tonight Show*. We never tired of Johnny because, like any good Midwesterner, he was always a polite visitor in our homes. Carson was the perfect late-night house guest: charming, easy-going, witty, and we could turn him off whenever we felt like it.

Reflecting on his childhood, Johnny observed, "In a small Midwestern town, everybody knows everybody."

Maybe that's why the good-neighbor policy blows across the prairie like a welcome summer breeze.

Kindness is the language which
the deaf can hear and the blind can see.

Mark Twain

Be fair. It pays, not only as moral imperative,
but also as common sense.

Harold Washington

Scatter seeds of kindness.

George Ade

Share the good fortune with others.

Paul Newman

Am I not destroying my enemies
when I make friends of them?

Abraham Lincoln

Never, never, never
be a cynic,
even a gentle one.

Vachel Lindsay

Tact is the ability to describe others
as they see themselves.

Abraham Lincoln

When I'm getting ready to reason with a man,
I spend one-third of my time thinking about
myself and what I am going to say —
and two-thirds thinking about him and
what he is going to say.

Abraham Lincoln

Nothing so needs reforming
as other people's habits.

Mark Twain

He has a right to criticize who has
a heart to help.

Abraham Lincoln

It is almost impossible to throw dirt on
someone without getting a little on yourself.

Abraham Lincoln

The love we give away is the only love
we keep.

Elbert Hubbard

Most people think in terms of getting.
Success, however, begins with giving.

Henry Ford

Love is the most precious thing in all the
world. Whatever figures in second place
doesn't even come close.

Ann Landers

Your friend is the one who knows
all about you and still likes you.

Elbert Hubbard

Youthful friendships are among
the greatest things in life.

John Dos Passos

Civilization is a method of living, an attitude
of equal respect for all men.

Jane Addams

The best index to a person's character
is how he treats people who can't do him
any good, and how he treats people
who can't fight back.

Abigail Van Buren

It is very easy to forgive others their
mistakes; it takes more grit and gumption to
forgive them for having witnessed your own.

Jessamyn West

Love cures people — both the ones
who give it and the ones who receive it.

Karl Menninger

Trust everybody, but cut the cards.

Finley Peter Dunne

Anger blows out the lamp of the mind.

Robert Ingersoll

Anyone who angers you conquers you.

Mother's Advice to Sister Elizabeth Kenny

Prejudice is a raft onto which
the shipwrecked mind clambers
and paddles to safety.

Ben Hecht

Virtue knows no color lines.

Ida B. Wells

To get the full value
of joy, you have
to have someone
to divide it with.

Mark Twain

<u>11</u>

Adversity

Susan Glaspell was born in Davenport, Iowa. After studying at Drake University in Des Moines, she began a successful career as a playwright and novelist. Glaspell wrote, "From those who have never sailed come the quickest and harshest judgements on bad seamanship in harsh seas."

The quotations in this chapter are selected for those times when we must sail through life's choppy waters. If you're experiencing tough times, batten down the hatches, full speed ahead, all hands on deck ... and don't forget to turn the page.

Only after many trials for strength,
only when all stimulants fail, does the
aspiring soul by its own sheer power
find the divine by resting upon itself.

Edgar Lee Masters

There are some things you learn best
in calm, and some in storm.

Willa Cather

You may not realize it when it happens,
but a kick in the teeth can be the best thing
in the world for you.

Walt Disney

You never know what you can do without
until you try.

Franklin Pierce Adams

Every adversity carries with it the seed
of an equal or greater benefit.

W. Clement Stone

Everything good that has happened to me
has happened as a direct result
of something bad.

Harry Caray

It's no use to grumble and complain,
It's just as cheap and easy to rejoice;
When God sorts out the weather
and sends rain —
Why, rain's my choice.

James Whitcomb Riley

At times like these it helps to recall there
have always been times like these.

Paul Harvey

When you get hurt, use it.

Ernest Hemingway

The one common denominator in the lives
of successful men is this: They get up
when they fall down.

Paul Harvey

People are not remembered by how
few times they fail, but by how often they
succeed. Every wrong step is
another step forward.

Thomas Edison

Trouble is the common denominator
of living, and it can be a blessing. Problems
act like a grindstone to smooth and polish us.

Ann Landers

Failure is instructive. We should learn as
much from our failures as from our successes.

John Dewey

When something angers you, you're face to face with opportunity.

Earl Nightingale

Some men storm
imaginary Alps all
their lives and die in
the foothills cursing
difficulties which
do not exist.

Edgar Watson Howe

I am an old man and have known a great many troubles, but most of them never happened.

Mark Twain

It's easy to be independent when you've got
money. But to be independent when you
haven't got a thing — that's the Lord's test.

Mahalia Jackson

Don't get too high or too low.
Mental consistency, stability, equilibrium —
in a word, balance — will allow you to adjust
to hard times and stay even during
the good times.

Dave Winfield

God will not look you over for medals,
degrees or diplomas, but for scars.

Elbert Hubbard

If you can't stand the heat, you'd better
get out of the kitchen.

Harry S. Truman

Suffering is one of the ways of knowing
you're alive.

Jessamyn West

It's not what they take away from you
that counts. It's what you do with
what you have left.

Hubert H. Humphrey

Life is about having to change
and making the best of it, without knowing
what's going to happen next.

Gilda Radner

No matter how good you're running —
or how bad you're running — finish the race.

Alan Kulwicki

No one would have crossed the ocean
if he could have gotten off the ship
in the storm.

Charles F. Kettering

It is best not to swap horses
while crossing the river.

Abraham Lincoln

Every man's got to figure
to get beat sometimes.

Joe Louis

A genius is a man who takes the lemons
that fate hands him and starts
a lemonade stand.

Elbert Hubbard

When you have got an elephant
by the hind leg, and he is trying to run away,
it's best to let him run.

Abraham Lincoln

Being poor is a frame of mind.

Mike Todd

If you want a place in the sun, you've got
to put up with a few blisters.

Abigail Van Buren

I personally think we developed language
because of our deep need to complain.

Lily Tomlin

It's always something.

Father's Advice to Gilda Radner

12

Hard Work

In 1856, a nineteen-year-old named Marshall Field moved to Chicago and took a job as a clerk in a mercantile store. Only nine years later, he co-founded the firm which bore his name. By the turn of the century, Field's department stores were producing over $40,000,000 a year in revenues, a staggering amount in those days.

Marshall Field had simple advice for young men and women entering the workplace. He warned, "Beware a misfit occupation." The quotations in this chapter examine the rewards of a well-chosen profession.

We all do our best work when it seems like play. In that magic moment when vocation becomes avocation, miracles begin to happen.

Never continue in a job you don't enjoy.
If you're happy in what you're doing you'll
like yourself. And that, along with physical
health, makes you a success.

Johnny Carson

When you love something,
you don't consider it work.
You can do a lot on love.

Mike Ilitch

Nothing is work unless you'd rather
be doing something else.

George Halas

Work for your soul's sake.

Edgar Lee Masters

Work hard. There is no short-cut.

Alfred P. Sloan, Jr.

Luck is a dividend of sweat.
The more you sweat, the luckier you get.

Ray Kroc

Whenever I got ready to call it a day,
I'd think, "No, somebody else is practicing."

Larry Bird

Even a "natural" has to practice hard.

Joe Louis

Keep on going and chances are you'll
stumble on something, perhaps when you
least expect it. But you'll never stumble
on something sitting down.

Charles F. Kettering

The best preparation for good work
tomorrow is to do good work today.

Elbert Hubbard

The best thing I've learned in life is
that things have to be worked for. There's no
magic in making a winning team,
but there's plenty of work.

Knute Rockne

Labor disgraces no man.
Unfortunately you occasionally find
some men who disgrace labor.

Ulysses S. Grant

A lot of people do not recognize opportunity because it usually goes around wearing overalls and looking like hard work.

Thomas Edison

None of my inventions came by accident. They came by work.

Thomas Edison

Genius is one percent inspiration and ninety-nine percent perspiration.

Thomas Edison

Men have never fully used their powers
because they have waited upon some power
external to themselves to do the work
they are responsible for doing.

John Dewey

Discover creative solitude.

Carl Sandburg

Even if a farmer intends to loaf,
he gets up in time to get an early start.

Edgar Watson Howe

When I stand before God
at the end of my life, I
would hope that I would
not have a single bit of
talent left and could say,
"I used everything
You gave me."

Erma Bombeck

13

Business Advice

In 1732, Thomas Fuller, M.D. wrote, "Boldness in business is the first, second, and third thing." Dr. Fuller would have appreciated the management style of General Robert E. Wood. As president of Sears, Roebuck and Company, General Wood approached his work with a military flair. He once observed, "Business is like war in one respect. If its grand strategy is correct, any number of tactical errors can be made, and yet the enterprise proves successful."

The quotations in this chapter will help you become a better business tactician. Once you've developed your grand strategy, the rest is simple; just work hard, be bold, and await the spoils.

Opportunity is limited only by imagination.
Charles F. Kettering

These are really good times,
but only a few people know it.
Henry Ford

One machine can do the work
of fifty ordinary men. No machine can do
the work of one extraordinary man.
Elbert Hubbard

You're only as good as the people you hire.
Ray Kroc

We've never succeeded in making
a good deal with a bad person.
Warren Buffett

When two men in business always agree,
one of them is unnecessary.

William Wrigley, Jr.

If you aren't fired with enthusiasm,
you'll be fired with enthusiasm.

Vince Lombardi

Good fellows are a dime a dozen,
but an aggressive leader is priceless.

Red Blaik

Leadership is the ability to get people
to do what they don't want to do — and like it.

Harry S. Truman

A real executive goes around
with a worried look on his assistants.

Vince Lombardi

It is not the employer who pays the wages.
He only handles the money.
It is the product that pays the wages.

Henry Ford

Restlessness and discontent
are the first necessities of progress.

Thomas Edison

Money is like an arm or a leg.
Use it or lose it.

Henry Ford

It's far better to buy a wonderful company
at a fair price than a fair company
at a wonderful price.

Warren Buffett

A problem well stated
is a problem half solved.

Charles F. Kettering

If you need a piece of equipment
and don't buy it, you pay for it even though
you don't have it.

Henry Ford

Everything comes to him who hustles
while he waits.

Thomas Edison

It's no great sin to miss a great opportunity
outside one's area of competence.

Warren Buffett

Nothing is more vulnerable
than entrenched success.

George Romney

In every aspect of life, have a game plan,
and then do your best to achieve it.

Alan Kulwicki

Fight for quality.

Walt Disney

14

Freedom

Carl Sandburg was born to poor immigrant parents in Galesburg, Illinois. Seeing few happy prospects on the home front, young Carl traveled west to Kansas, where he earned his keep as a farm hand and dishwasher. After serving in the military, Sandburg discovered his towering talent for literature. The rest, as they say, is poetry.

Sandburg devoted much of his life to the study of Abraham Lincoln. Lincoln observed, "In giving freedom to the slave, we assure freedom to the free — honorable alike in what we give and what we preserve."

On the following pages Honest Abe and his fellow Midwesterners discuss America's greatest gift to her citizens: freedom. But freedom is much more than a gift. It is a privilege and a responsibility.

Carl Sandburg once noted, "Freedom is a habit." This habit, as Lincoln would be quick to remind us, is preserved only as long as it is shared.

The cause of civil liberty
must not be surrendered at the end of one
or even one hundred defeats.
The fight must go on.

Abraham Lincoln

Better to die fighting against injustice
than to die like a rat in a trap.

Ida B. Wells

Let the people know the truth
and the country is safe.

Abraham Lincoln

The man who does not do his own thinking
is a slave.

Robert Ingersoll

Restriction of free thought and free speech
is the most dangerous of subversions.

William O. Douglas

Those who deny freedom
to others deserve it not
for themselves.

Abraham Lincoln

You cannot help men permanently
    by doing for them what they could and
        should do for themselves.

Abraham Lincoln

Self government won't work
        without self-discipline.

Paul Harvey

Freedom is a tenable objective only
        for responsible individuals.

Milton Friedman

The right to work is
    the most precious liberty men possess.

William O. Douglas

There's no such thing as a free lunch.

Milton Friedman

The right to be left alone is indeed
the beginning of all freedoms.

William O. Douglas

This is the penalty of democracy —
that we are bound to move forward
or retrograde together.

Jane Addams

Moral progress comes not
in comfortable and complacent times, but
out of trial and confusion.

Gerald Ford

It is better to lose the election
than to mislead the people.

Adlai Stevenson

The impersonal hand of government can never replace the helping hand of a neighbor.

Hubert H. Humphrey

15

Observations on Farming, Cleaning, Schooling, and Other Necessities of Life

W. Clement Stone noted, "There is very little difference in people, but that little difference makes a big difference. The little difference is attitude."

We conclude with a potpourri of wisdom designed to lift your spirits and improve your attitude. Enjoy.

A miracle occurs
at the moment our eyes
can see and our ears hear
what is there about
us always.

Willa Cather

I don't know who my grandfather was.
I'm much more concerned to know
what his grandson will be.

Abraham Lincoln

When in doubt, tell the truth.

Mark Twain

There are several good protections against
temptation, but the surest is cowardice.

Mark Twain

A retentive memory may be a good thing,
but the ability to forget is the true token
of greatness.

Elbert Hubbard

Nobody ever forgets
where he buried the hatchet.

Kin Hubbard

Few things are harder to put up with than
the annoyance of a good example.

Mark Twain

A bore is a person who talks
when you want him to listen.

Ambrose Bierce

A lawsuit is a machine you go into as a pig
and come out as a sausage.

Ambrose Bierce

Cleaning your house while your kids
are still growing is like shoveling the walk
before it stops snowing.

Phyllis Diller

No problem is so big or so complicated
that it can't be run away from.

Linus

Cartoon Character by Charles Schulz

Time wounds all heels.

Jane Ace

The perils of duck hunting are great,
especially for the duck.

Walter Cronkite

If God didn't want man to hunt,
he wouldn't have given us plaid shirts.

Johnny Carson

I base my fashion taste on what doesn't itch.

Gilda Radner

People who fight fire
with fire usually
end up with ashes.

Abigail Van Buren

The first quality of a good education is good manners.

Hubert H. Humphrey

Few men own their own property.
The property owns them.

Robert Ingersoll

About the only thing on a farm that has
an easy time is the dog.

Edgar Watson Howe

Most of us grew up poor and didn't know it.
Today, if you're poor, the government
never lets you forget it.

Paul Harvey

Old habits are strong and jealous.

Dorthea Brande

My best friend is the one who brings out
the best in me.

Henry Ford

Always select the right sort of parents.

George Ade

Flattery is all right — if you don't inhale.

Adlai Stevenson

If humility speaks of itself, it is gone.

D. L. Moody

Women are less ashamed than men.
They have less to be ashamed of.

Ambrose Bierce

Never lend your car to anyone to whom
you have given birth.

Erma Bombeck

Man does not live by words alone,
although he sometimes must eat them.

Adlai Stevenson

There is more treasure
in books than in all
the pirates' loot
on Treasure Island.

Walt Disney

Go to school. I'd be better off if I had gone
to school and so will you.

Joe Louis

The physician can bury his mistakes,
but the architect can only advise his client
to plant vines.

Frank Lloyd Wright

The White House is the finest jail in the world.

Harry S. Truman

There is no economy in buying cheap
equipment. Buy only the best.

Knute Rockne

Opportunity is limitless.
Where there is an
open mind, there will
always be a frontier.

Charles F. Kettering

Sources